Help the Environment

Reusing and Recycling

Revised Edition

Charlotte Guillain

heinemann
raintree

To contact Capstone Global Library please call 800-747-4992 or visit our website www.mycapstone.com

Picture research: Erica Martin, Hannah Taylor and Ginny Stroud-Lewis
Designed by Philippa Jenkins

Library of Congress Cataloging-in-Publication Data
Guillain, Charlotte.
Reusing and recycling revised edition / Charlotte Guillain.
p. cm. -- (Help the environment)
Includes bibliographical references and index.
ISBN-13: 978-1-4329-0888-1 (hc)
ISBN-13: 978-1-4846-3566-7 (pb)
ISBN-13: 978-1-4846-0081-8 (Saddle Stitch)
1. Recycling (Waste, etc.)--Juvenile literature. I. Title.
TD792.G85 2008
363.72'82--dc22
2007041173

Acknowledgments
The author and publisher would like to thank the following for permission to reproduce photographs: Corbis: Ocean/68, 19; iStockphoto: fcafotodigital, 14, 20 (bottom left), SupharoekBK, 10; Pearson Education Ltd: 6, 7, 8, 9, 20 (top left & top right), 23 (bottom); Shutterstock: blvdone, 4 (bottom left), Carlos Horta, 12, Evan Lorne, 17, Hurst Photo, back cover, 21, James R. Martin, 15, 23 (middle), Matej Kastelic, 22, Miks Mihails Ignats, 4 (top right), 23 (top), Monkey Business Images, 5, Rosomak, 4 (bottom right), RTimages, 13, 20 (bottom right), sunsetman, cover, szefei, 4 (top left), Teresa Kasprzycka, 11, Tyler Olson, 16, 18

Printed and bound in the United States.
011217 010225RP

Help the Environment

Reusing and Recycling

Revised Edition

Acorn

Contents

What Is the Environment?

The environment is the world all around us.

We need to care for
the environment.

How Can We Reuse Things?

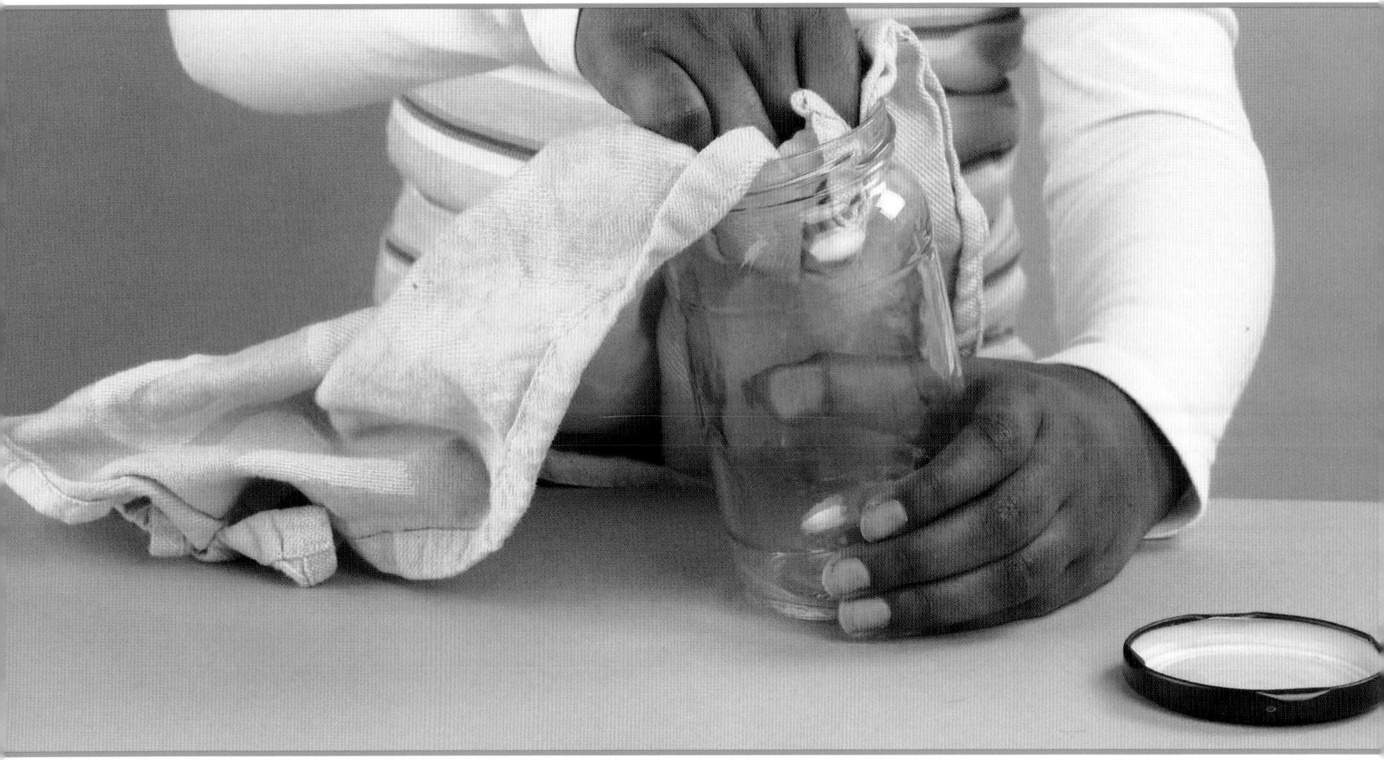

When we use old things
again, we reuse them.

When we reuse things,
we do not make trash.
We help the environment.

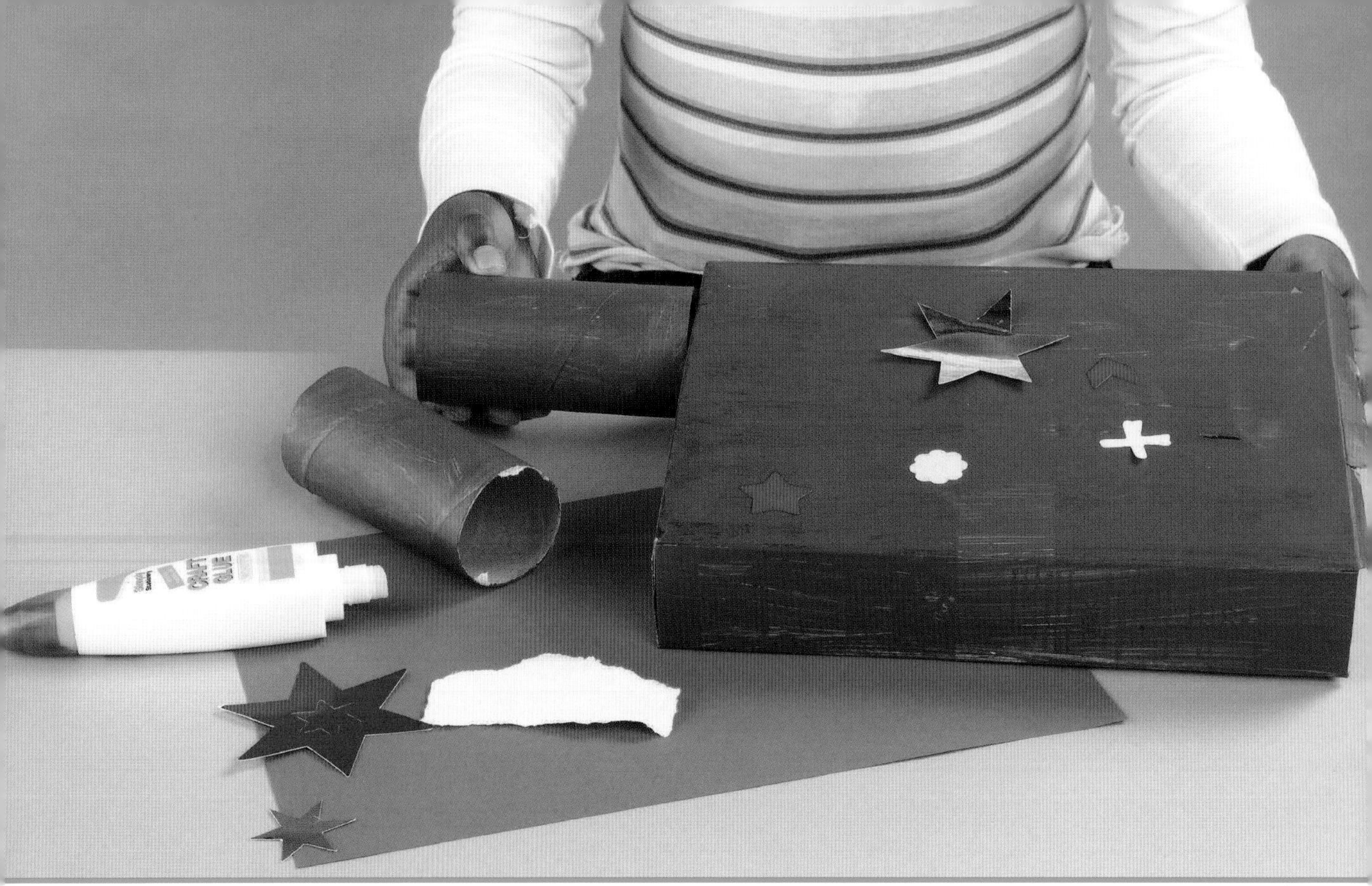

When we reuse boxes,

we do not waste boxes.

We help the environment.

When we reuse paper,
we do not waste paper.
We help the environment.

How Can We Recycle Things?

When we make new things from old things, we recycle them.

When we recycle things,
we do not waste them.
We help the environment.

We use glass for many things.

When we recycle glass,
we do not waste glass.
We help the environment.

We use plastic for many things.

When we recycle plastic,
we do not waste plastic.
We help the environment.

We use paper for many things.

When we recycle paper,
we do not waste paper.
We help the environment.

We use metal for many things.

When we recycle metal,
we do not waste metal.
We help the environment.

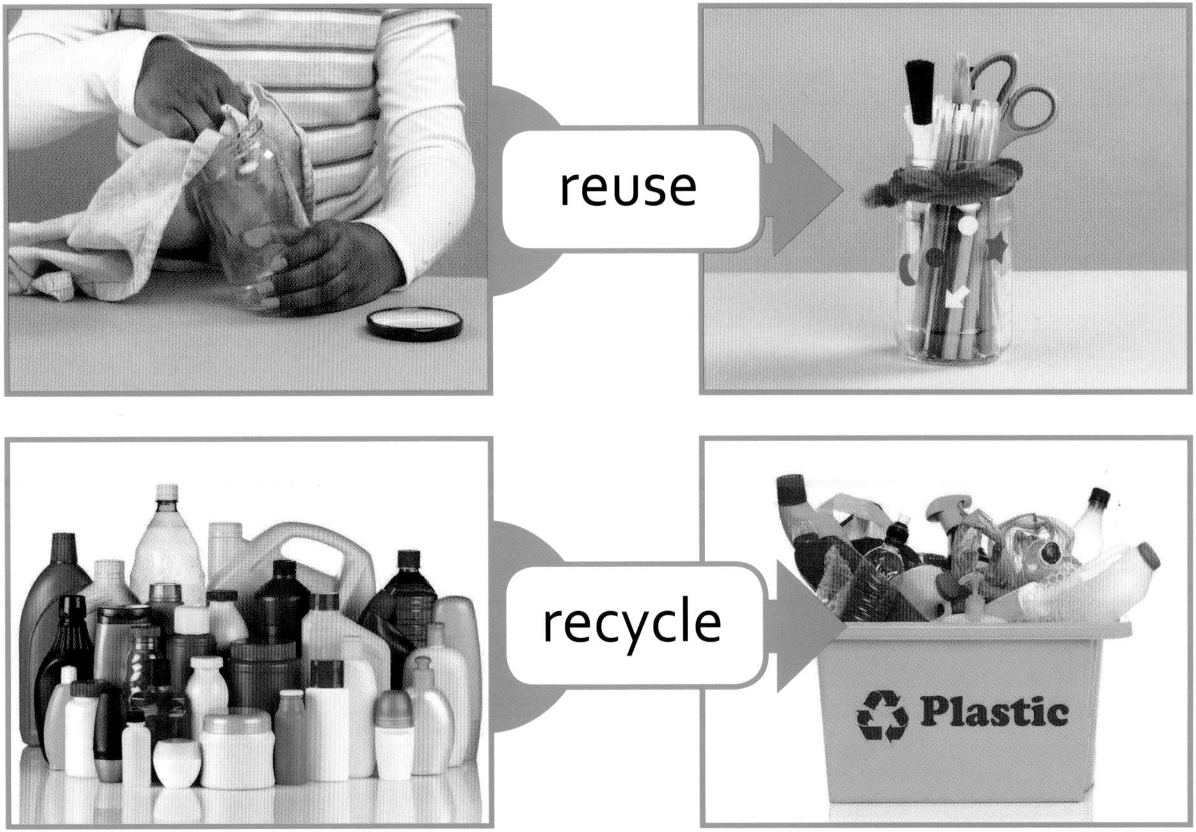

We can reuse and recycle every day.

We can help the environment.

How Are They Helping?

How are these people reusing things?

Answer on p. 24

Picture Glossary

environment the world around us

recycle make old things into new things

reuse use again

Index

Answer to question on p.22: These people are buying old things so that they can use them again.

Note to Parents and Teachers

Before reading
Talk to children about reusing and recycling. Explain how it helps the environment. Show them a sock that is too small for them to wear. What suggestions can they come up with for reusing (stuffing a soft toy, making a sock puppet)? Ask children to think about things that they can recycle, such as drink cans and paper.

After reading
- Ask children to bring in any material that can be reused to make something new (used foil, egg cartons,newspaper or used construction paper, fabric, etc.). Draw a very large outline of an animal, such as a lion or a dinosaur. Help children cut up some of the material and decide where to place it on the outline to make a collage picture.